100 facts
Mammals

100 facts
Mammals

Jinny Johnson
Consultant: Steve Parker

Miles
KeLLy

First published in 2001 by Miles Kelly Publishing Ltd
Harding's Barn, Bardfield End Green, Thaxted, Essex, CM6 3PX, UK

This edition updated 2015, printed 2016

8 10 12 14 15 13 11 9 7

Publishing Director Belinda Gallagher
Creative Director Jo Cowan
Editorial Director Rosie Neave
Designers Rob Hale, Andrea Slane
Image Manager Liberty Newton
Production Elizabeth Collins, Caroline Kelly
Reprographics Stephan Davis, Jennifer Cozens, Thom Allaway
Indexer Jane Parker
Assets Lorraine King

ISBN 978-1-78209-591-0

Printed in China

British Library Cataloguing-in-Publication Data
A catalogue record for this book is available from the British Library

ACKNOWLEDGEMENTS

The publishers would like to thank the following sources for the use of their photographs:
Key: t = top, b = bottom, l = left, r = right, c = centre, bg = background

Cover (front) Moodboard/Photoshot; (back) Thomas Barrat/Shutterstock.com
Corbis 35(b) Tom Brakefield; 44 Ocean **FLPA** 15(b) Norbert Wu/Minden Pictures; 26(t) Imagebroker,
Konrad Wothe; 27(b) ImageBroker/Imagebroker; 33(br) Mark Newman; 37(c) Yann Hubert/Biosphoto;
39(b) Michael Durham/Minden Pictures; 45 John Eveson **Glow Images** 14(c) SuperStock; 25(b) Terry
Whittaker/FLPA; 38 Juniors Bildarchiv; 42(cl) Rolf Nussbaumer **National Geographic Creative** 10(l) Hiroya
Minakuchi/Minden Pictures; 17(c) Tim Laman; 33(b) Nicole Duplaix **Nature Picture Library** 6–7 T.J. Rich;
29(t) Andy Rouse; 29(b) Jabruson; 31(r) Jabruson; 34(tr) Jim Clare **Photoshot** 21(c) Imago
Shutterstock.com 2–3 CHAINFOTO24; 5(b) Victor Shova; 8 Norma Cornes; 9(t) BMJ; 9(tc) Smileus;
9(b) Incredible Arctic; 11(b) CHAINFOTO24; 12(bl) Neil Burton; 12(c) Mark Beckwith; 14–15(c) jaytee;
16–17(c) Sarun T; 18(c) Incredible Arctic; 18(b) Magdanatka; 19(b) Zoltan Katona; 23(t) Erni;
24(t) outdoorsman; 24(b) EcoPrint; 26–27 Bozena Fulawka; 28(b) Mogens Trolle; 30(b) Ultrashock;
32(tr) BMJ; 32–33 theerapol sri-in; 33(tl) Eric Isselee; 39(t) TranceDrumer; 40–41(b) Anna Omelchenko;
41(t) worldswildlifewonders; 42(b) EcoPrint; 43(b) Andrea Izzotti; 47(b) Jean-Edouard Rozey
Science Photo Library 37(b) Thomas & Pat Leeson

All other photographs are from:
DigitalSTOCK, digitalvision, John Foxx, PhotoAlto, PhotoDisc, PhotoEssentials, PhotoPro, Stockbyte

Every effort has been made to acknowledge the source and copyright holder of each picture.
Miles Kelly Publishing apologises for any unintentional errors or omissions.

Made with paper from a sustainable forest

www.mileskelly.net
info@mileskelly.net

Contents

What are mammals?

1 Mammals are warm-blooded animals with a bony skeleton and fur or hair. Being warm-blooded means that a mammal keeps its body at a constant temperature, even if the weather is very cold. The skeleton supports the body and protects the delicate parts inside, such as the heart, lungs and brain. There is one sort of mammal you know very well, it's you!

▼▶ Two western lowland gorillas meet face to face. Gorillas are highly intelligent mammals and close cousins of humans.

Mammal groups

2 There are nearly 5500 different types of mammal. Most mammals have babies that grow inside the mother's body. While a baby mammal grows, a special organ called a placenta supplies it with food and oxygen from the mother's body. These mammals are called placental mammals.

Placental mammals

Placenta

Birth canal

▲ A baby elephant in the womb receives nourishment through the placenta.

3 Not all mammals' young develop inside the mother's body. Two smaller groups of mammals do things differently. Monotremes, such as platypuses and echidnas (spiny anteaters), lay eggs. The platypus lays her eggs in a burrow, but the echidna keeps her single egg in a special pouch in her belly until it is ready to hatch.

▶ The echidna keeps her egg in a pouch until it hatches after about ten days.

Monotremes

4 Mammal mothers feed their babies on milk from their own bodies. The baby sucks this milk from teats on special mammary glands, also called udders or breasts, on the mother's body. The milk contains all the food the young animal needs to help it grow.

5 Marsupials give birth to tiny young that finish developing in a pouch. A baby kangaroo is only 2 centimetres long when it is born. Tiny, blind and hairless, it makes its own way to the safety of its mother's pouch. Once there, it latches onto a teat in the pouch and begins to feed.

A joey starts life as a tiny undeveloped baby

Marsupials

▲ A baby kangaroo is called a joey. It stays in the pouch for about six months while it grows.

▼ This reindeer uses its eyes, ears and especially nose to sense the world.

6 Most mammals have good senses of sight, smell and hearing. Their senses help them watch out for enemies, find food and keep in touch with each other. For many mammals, smell is their most important sense. Plant-eaters such as rabbits and deer sniff the air to pick up scents of danger, especially those of predators.

I DON'T BELIEVE IT!

Lemmings are very fast breeders. Females can become pregnant at only 14 days old, and they can produce litters of as many as 12 young every month.

Big and small

BLUE WHALE
33.5 metres long

► In summer a blue whale eats up to 4 tonnes of food daily, reaching its greatest weight of over 150 tonnes.

7 The blue whale is the biggest mammal, and one of the largest animals ever known to have lived. It can measure as long as seven family cars parked end to end, and spends all of its life in the ocean.

ELEPHANT
4 metres tall

► Elephants may eat more than 300 kilograms of leaves, twigs and fruit each day.

8 The elephant is the biggest land mammal. There are three kinds of elephant – the African savannah elephant, the African forest elephant, and the Asian. The African savannah elephant is the biggest – a full-grown male may weigh as much as 10 tonnes – more than 100 adult people.

GORILLA
1.75 metres tall

▼ A full-grown male gorilla weighs up to 275 kilograms.

9 Gorillas are the biggest primates. Primates are the group of mammals to which chimpanzees and humans belong.

GIRAFFE
5.5 metres tall

▼ The giraffe's height helps it reach juicy leaves at the tops of trees.

10 The giraffe is the tallest animal, as well as mammal. A male is as tall as three or four people standing on each other's shoulders. Giraffes lives in Africa, south of the Sahara desert.

11 The capybara is the largest rodent. Rodents are the group of mammals that include rats and mice. It lives around ponds, lakes and rivers in South America.

CAPYBARA
1.3 metres long

▲ A well-fed capybara weighs over 70 kilograms.

MOUSE DEER
85 cm long

▲ The mouse deer is just 30 centimetres in height.

12 The tiny mouse deer is the size of a hare. Also know as the chevrotain, it lives in African forests.

13 The smallest mammal is the tiny hog-nosed bat. A full-grown adult weighs less than a teaspoon of rice!

HOG-NOSED BAT
3 centimetres long

► The tiny hog-nosed bat is just 2 grams in weight.

Fast movers

14 The cheetah can run faster than any other animal. It can move at about 100 kilometres an hour, but it cannot run this fast for long. The cheetah uses its speed to catch other animals to eat. It creeps towards its prey until it is only about 100 metres away. Then it races towards it at top speed, ready for the final attack.

15 The pronghorn is slower than the cheetah, but can run for longer. It can keep up a speed of 70 kilometres an hour for about ten minutes.

▶ The cheetah's long slender legs and muscular body help it to run fast. The long tail balances the body while it is running.

16 Even the brown hare can run at more than 70 kilometres an hour. Its powerful back legs help it move fast enough to escape enemies such as foxes.

◀ For each stride, the brown hare kicks hard backwards with its long rear legs.

SPEED DEMONS!

Ask an adult to measure how far in metres you can run in 10 seconds. Multiply this by 6, and then times the answer by 60 to find out how many metres you can run in an hour. If you divide this by 1000 you will get your speed in kilometres per hour. You will find it will be far less than the cheetah's 100 kilometres an hour!

◀ The red kangaroo can leap 9 or 10 metres in a single bound.

17 The red kangaroo is a champion jumper. It can leap along at 40 kilometres an hour or more. The kangaroo needs to be able to travel fast. It lives in the dry desert lands of Australia and often has to journey long distances to find grass to eat and water to drink.

Swimmers and divers

18 Most swimming mammals have flippers and fins instead of legs. Their bodies have become sleek and streamlined to help them move through the water easily. Seals and sea lions have large, paddle-like flippers that they can use to drag themselves along on land, as well as for swimming power in water. Whales never come to land. They swim by moving their tails up and down and using their front flippers to steer.

▲ The humpback has the largest flippers of any whale, at 5 metres long.

QUIZ

1. How deep can a Weddell seal dive?

2. What is the layer of fat on a seal's body called?

3. How fast can a killer whale swim?

Answers:
1. 750 metres or more
2. Blubber 3. 55 kilometers an hour

19 The killer whale can reach a speed of 55 kilometres an hour. A fierce hunter, it uses its speed to chase fast-swimming prey such as squid, fish and seals. It sometimes hunts in groups and will even attack other whales. Killer whales live in all the world's oceans. Despite their name, they are the largest of the dolphin family. They grow up to 10 metres long and weigh as much as 9 tonnes.

◄ Killer whales often leap clear of the water, an action known as breaching.

▼ A mother and baby Weddell seal. The Weddell is a big seal — 3.5 metres long and half a tonne in weight.

20 The Weddell seal can dive deeper than any other seal. It goes down to depths of 750 metres or more in its search for cod and other fish. This seal can stay underwater for a long while, and dives of more than an hour have been timed. It lives in the icy waters of Antarctica, and its body is covered with a thick layer of fatty blubber that helps to keep it warm.

Fliers and gliders

21 Bats are the only true flying mammals. They zoom through the air on wings made of skin. These are attached to the sides of their body and supported by specially adapted, extra-long bones of the arms and hands and fingers. Bats generally hunt at night. During the day they hang upside down by their feet from a branch or cave ledge. Their wings are neatly folded at their sides or around their body.

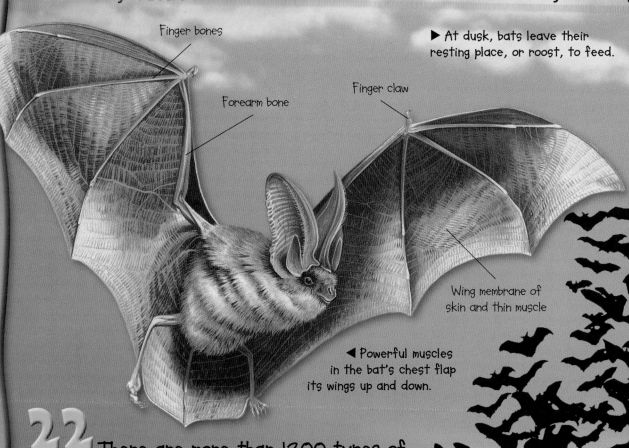

Finger bones

Forearm bone

Finger claw

▶ At dusk, bats leave their resting place, or roost, to feed.

Wing membrane of skin and thin muscle

◀ Powerful muscles in the bat's chest flap its wings up and down.

22 There are more than 1200 types of bat. They live in most parts of the world, but not in colder areas. Bats feed on many different sorts of food. Most common are the insect-eating bats, which snatch their prey from the air while in flight. Others feast on pollen and nectar from flowers. Flesh-eating bats catch fish, birds, lizards and frogs.

23 Flying lemurs don't really fly – they just glide from tree to tree. They can glide distances of up to 100 metres with the help of flaps of skin at the sides of the body. When the flying lemur takes off from a branch it holds its limbs out, stretching the skin flaps so that they act like a parachute.

▼ The skin flaps of the flying lemur, or colugo, are not only along the sides, but also between the rear legs and tail.

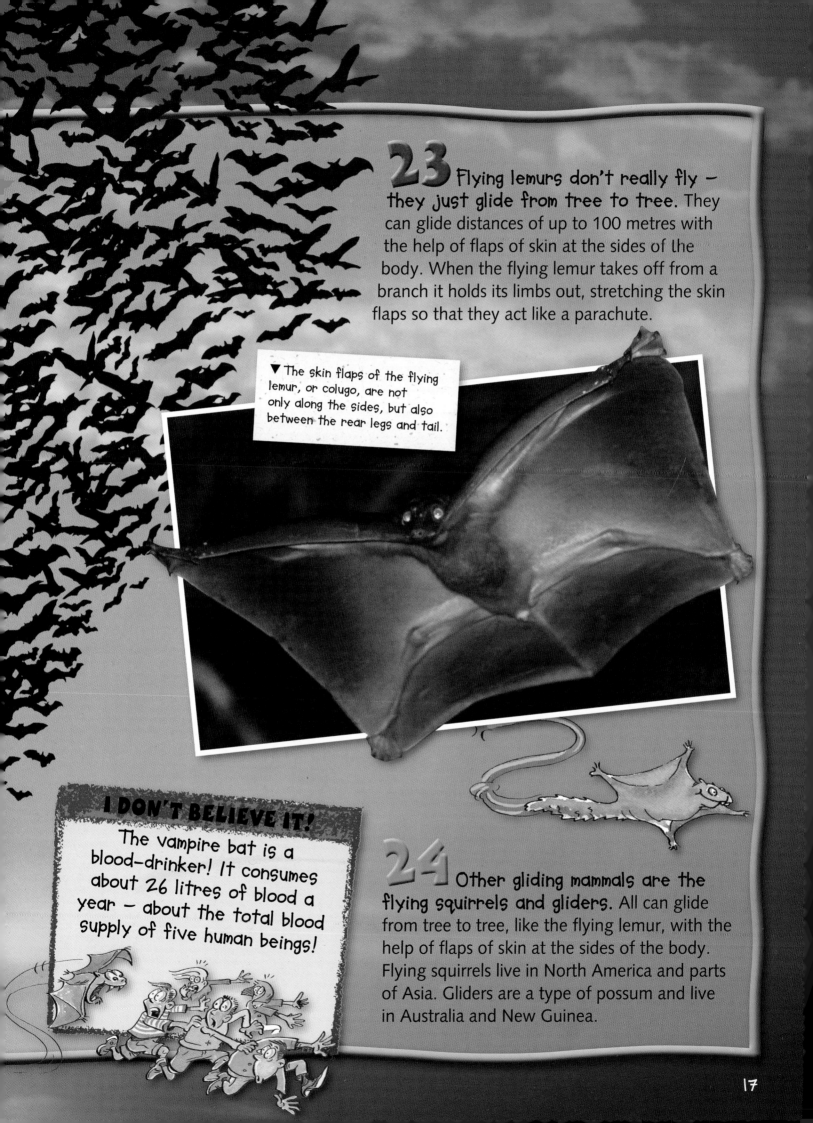

I DON'T BELIEVE IT!
The vampire bat is a blood-drinker! It consumes about 26 litres of blood a year – about the total blood supply of five human beings!

24 Other gliding mammals are the flying squirrels and gliders. All can glide from tree to tree, like the flying lemur, with the help of flaps of skin at the sides of the body. Flying squirrels live in North America and parts of Asia. Gliders are a type of possum and live in Australia and New Guinea.

Life in snow and ice

25 **The polar bear is the biggest land predator.** This Arctic hunter can run fast, swim well and even dive under the ice to hunt its main prey – seals. It also catches seabirds and land animals such as the Arctic hare and reindeer.

▶ The polar bear's thick, white fur helps to keep it warm – even the soles of its feet are furry.

26 **Caribou, also known as reindeer, feed in Arctic lands.** The land around the Arctic Ocean is called the tundra. In the short summer, plenty of plants grow, the caribou eat their fill and give birth to their young. When summer is over, the caribou trek up to 1000 kilometres south to spend the winter in forests.

27 **Some Arctic animals such as the Arctic hare and the ermine, or stoat, change colour.** In winter these animals have white fur, which helps them hide among the snow. In summer, when white fur would make them very easy to spot, their coats turn brown.

◀ Reindeer scrape and nose into snow to find plants to eat.

28 The Arctic ground squirrel digs its own burrow system to shelter in, or renovates an old, unoccupied set of burrows. It lines the main nest area with dry grass, moss and thin stems. Here it hibernates for half the year or more – from August to the following April.

29 The leopard seal is one of the fiercest hunters in the Antarctic. It lives in the waters around Antarctica and preys on penguins, fish and other seals. There are no land mammals in the Antarctic.

▲ After waking from hibernation, plants, seeds and berries make up the diet of the Arctic ground squirrel

30 The walrus has tusks that grow as much as one metre long. They are used to drag itself out of water and onto the ice as well as for defending itself against enemies and for display against rival walruses.

31 The musk ox has a long shaggy outer coat to help it survive the Arctic cold. A thick undercoat keeps out the damp. The musk ox eats grass, moss and lichen. In winter it digs through the snow with its hooves to reach its food.

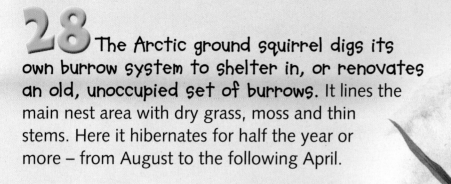

▼ Huge male musk ox head–butt to control the herd.

Creatures of the night

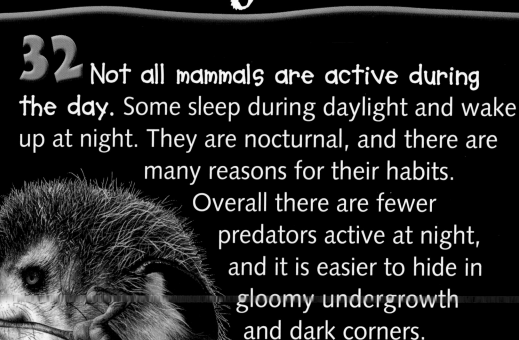

32 Not all mammals are active during the day. Some sleep during daylight and wake up at night. They are nocturnal, and there are many reasons for their habits. Overall there are fewer predators active at night, and it is easier to hide in gloomy undergrowth and dark corners.

33 The aye-aye is a strange tree-dwelling lemur of Madagascar. Like many nocturnal animals it has large eyes to collect as much light as possible. It sleeps by day in a nest of leaves and twigs and searches at night for grubs and other small creatures, using its very long fourth finger to pull them from under bark.

▲ An aye-aye probes into holes in trunks and branches for food.

QUIZ

1. What word describes animals that are active at night?

2. Where does the aye-aye live?

3. What does the red panda eat?

Answers:
1. Nocturnal 2. Madagascar
3. Bamboo shoots, fruit, acorns, insects, birds' eggs

34 **The red panda is a night feeder.** It sleeps during the day, but at night it searches for food such as bamboo shoots, roots, fruit and acorns. It also eats insects, birds' eggs and small animals. In summer, red pandas sometimes wake in the day to climb trees to find fresh leaves to eat.

35 **Hyenas usually come out at night to find food.** They hunt their own prey and are also scavangers – they feed on the remains of creatures killed by larger hunters. When a lion has eaten its fill, hyenas rush in to grab the remains.

36 **Bats hunt at night.** Insect feeders, such as the horseshoe bat, manage to find their prey by means of a special kind of animal sonar. The bat makes high-pitched squeaks as it flies. If the waves from these sounds hit an animal, such as a moth, echoes bounce back to the bat. These echoes tell the bat where its prey is.

◀ Hyenas hunt at night using their excellent sense of smell.

Busy builders

37 Beavers build their home by damming a stream with branches, stones and mud. This creates a deep lake where they can make a winter food store and a shelter called a lodge. Once the dam is made, they begin to build the lodge, usually a dome-shaped structure made of sticks and mud.

▶ Beavers repair and strengthen their dam daily. In summer, they feed on twigs, leaves and roots. They collect extra branches and logs to store for winter.

Dam holds back water

38 The beaver is an excellent swimmer. It has a broad flat tail, which acts like a paddle when swimming, and it has webbed feet. It dives well, too, and can stay underwater for 15 minutes or more. To warn others of danger, a beaver may slap the water with its tail as it dives.

39 The harvest mouse makes a nest on grass stems. It winds some strong stems round one another to make a kind of platform. It then weaves softer grass stems into the structure to form a ball-like shape about 10 centimetres across.

▶ The female harvest mouse looks after as many as ten babies in her tennis ball-sized woven nest.

Dry living platform

Underwater entrance to lodge

Incisor teeth gnaw wood

Family life

40 Many mammals live alone, except when they have young, but others live in groups. Wolves live in family groups called packs. The pack is led by an adult female and her mate and may include up to 20 animals.

41 A type of mongoose called a meerkat lives in large groups of up to 30 animals. The group is called a colony and contains several family units of a pair of adults along with their young. The colony lives in a network of underground burrows. The members of the colony guard each other against enemies.

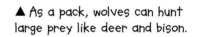

▲ As a pack, wolves can hunt large prey like deer and bison.

▼ Some meerkats watch for danger while others feed.

42 The male elephant seal fights rival males to gather a group of females. This group is called a harem and the male seal defends his females from other males. The group does not stay together for long after mating.

43 Some whales live in families too. Pilot whales, for example, live in groups of 20 or more animals that swim and hunt together. A group may include several adult males and a number of females and their young.

44 Naked mole rats live underground in a colony of animals led by one female. The colony includes about 100 animals and the ruling female, or queen, is the only one that produces young. Other colony members dig burrows to find food for the group, and look after the queen.

45 Lions live in groups called prides. The pride may include one or more adult males, females related to each other, and their young. The average number in a pride is 15. Female young generally stay with the pride of their birth but males must leave before they are full-grown. Lions are unusual in their family lifestyle – most other big cats live alone.

▼ Bonobos are generally peaceful, sharing food with each other.

46 Bonobos (pygmy chimpanzees) live in large groups, known as communities, of 80 or more. These are usually a mix of females, males and young. Within the community certain individuals are close friends and interact more than with others. These groups spend time together looking for food, grooming each other, and resting. Sometimes, the whole community gathers to travel, usually led by one or a few females, or to sleep.

25

Desert dwellers

47 Many desert animals burrow underground to escape the scorching heat. The North African gerbil stays hidden all day and comes out at night to eat seeds and insects. This gerbil is so well adapted to desert life that it never needs to drink.

▶ The North African gerbil gets all the liquid it needs from its food.

48 The large ears of the fennec fox help it to lose heat from its body. This fox lives in the North African desert. For its size, it has the largest ears of any dog or fox.

49 Pallas's cat lives in the Gobi Desert. It has thick, long fur to keep it warm in the cold Gobi winter. Pallas's cat lives alone, usually in a cave or a burrow, and hunts mice and birds.

▶ The fennec's huge ears can hear prey as tiny as ants.

50 A camel can last for weeks without drinking. It can manage on the liquid it gets from feeding on desert plants. But when it does find some water it drinks as much as 100 litres at one time. It does not store water in its hump, but it can store fat.

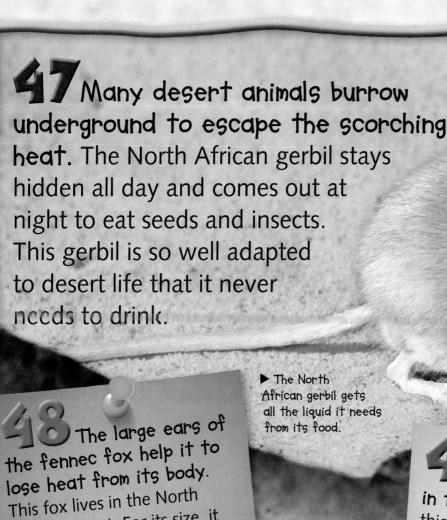

51
A kangaroo rat never needs to drink. The kidneys control how much water there is in an animal's body. The kangaroo rat's kidneys are much more efficient than ours. It can even make some of its food into water inside its body!

52
The bactrian camel has thick fur to keep it warm in winter. It lives in the Gobi Desert in Asia where winter weather can be very cold indeed. In summer, the camel's long shaggy fur drops off, leaving the camel almost hairless.

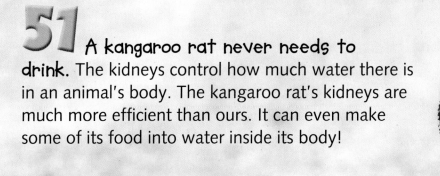

53
The desert hedgehog eats scorpions! It carefully nips off the scorpion's deadly sting before eating. It also eats insects and birds' eggs.

◀ The camel's hump fat is broken down into energy and water.

Backbone

Fat in hump

Blood supply

Intestines

Stomach

27

On the prowl

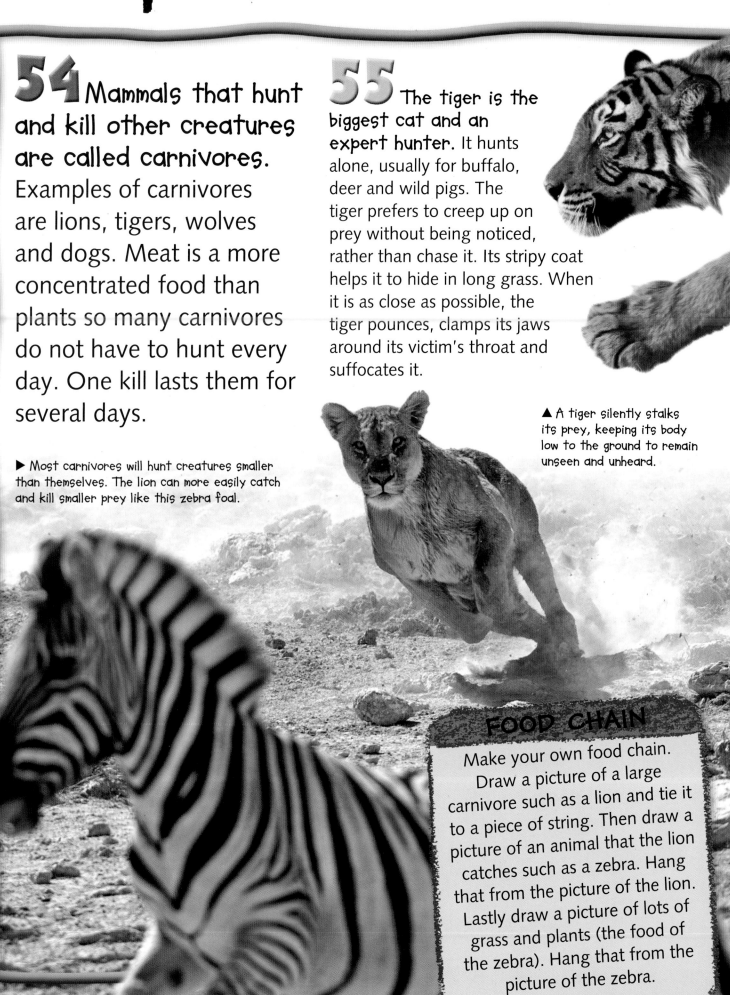

54 Mammals that hunt and kill other creatures are called carnivores. Examples of carnivores are lions, tigers, wolves and dogs. Meat is a more concentrated food than plants so many carnivores do not have to hunt every day. One kill lasts them for several days.

▶ Most carnivores will hunt creatures smaller than themselves. The lion can more easily catch and kill smaller prey like this zebra foal.

55 The tiger is the biggest cat and an expert hunter. It hunts alone, usually for buffalo, deer and wild pigs. The tiger prefers to creep up on prey without being noticed, rather than chase it. Its stripy coat helps it to hide in long grass. When it is as close as possible, the tiger pounces, clamps its jaws around its victim's throat and suffocates it.

▲ A tiger silently stalks its prey, keeping its body low to the ground to remain unseen and unheard.

FOOD CHAIN

Make your own food chain. Draw a picture of a large carnivore such as a lion and tie it to a piece of string. Then draw a picture of an animal that the lion catches such as a zebra. Hang that from the picture of the lion. Lastly draw a picture of lots of grass and plants (the food of the zebra). Hang that from the picture of the zebra.

56 Bears eat many different foods. They are carnivores but most, except for the polar bear, eat more plant material than meat. Brown bears eat fruit, nuts and insects and even catch fish. In summer, when salmon swim up rivers to lay their eggs, the bears wade into the shallows and hook fish with their huge paws.

57 Hunting dogs hunt in packs. Together, they can bring down a much larger animal. The pack sets off after a herd of plant-eaters such as zebras or gazelles. They try to separate one animal that is perhaps weaker or slower from the rest of the herd.

◄ This young wildebeest has been separated from its herd by a pack of African hunting dogs.

Fighting back

58 Some mammals have special ways of defending themselves from enemies. The nine-banded armadillo has body armour. Bony plates, topped with a layer of horn, cover the armadillo's back, sides and head.

59 The porcupine's body is covered with as many as 30,000 sharp spines. When an enemy approaches, the porcupine first rattles its spines as a warning. If this fails, the porcupine runs towards the attacker and drives the sharp spines into its flesh.

◄ The skunk's black-and-white-pattern is a warning that it can spray a horrible fluid.

▼ Its legs and belly are unprotected, but if attacked the armadillo rolls into tight ball.

Head and tail fit together to make an armoured 'ball'

Danger past, the armadillo begins to unfurl

The armadillo walks away

60 The skunk defends itself with a bad-smelling fluid. This fluid comes from special glands near the animal's tail. If threatened, the skunk lifts its tail and sprays its enemy. The fluid's strong smell irritates the victim's eyes and makes it hard to breathe, and the skunk runs away.

I DON'T BELIEVE IT!

Skunks sometimes feed on bees. They roll the bees on the ground to remove their stings before eating them.

61 **A rhinoceros may charge at its enemies at top speed.** Rhinos are generally peaceful animals but a female will defend her calf fiercely. If the calf is threatened, she will gallop towards the enemy with her head down and lunge with her sharp horns. Few predators will stay around to challenge an angry rhino.

◄ The sight of a full-grown rhinoceros charging is enough to make most predators turn and run.

62 **The pangolin's body is protected by tough overlapping scales.** These make the animal look like a giant pinecone. The pangolin feeds mainly on ants and termites and its thick scales protect it from the stinging bites of its tiny prey.

◄ Even the pangolin's long, prehensile (grasping) tail is well protected.

Deep in the jungle

63 Jungle mammals live at all levels of the forest from the tallest trees to the forest floor. Bats fly over the tree tops and monkeys and apes swing from branch to branch. Lower down, smaller creatures, such as civets and pottos, hide in the dense greenery.

▼ The Amazon rainforest echoes at dawn and dusk with howler monkey whoops and screeches.

64 The howler monkey has the loudest voice in the jungle. Each troop of howler monkeys has its own special area, called a territory. Males in rival troops shout at each other to defend their territory. Their shouts can be heard from nearly 5 kilometres away.

▼ Unlike most cats, jaguars like water, where they hunt for fish, turtles and snakes.

65 The jaguar is one of the fiercest hunters in the jungle. It lives in the South American rainforest and is the largest cat in South America. The pig-like peccary and the capybara – a large jungle rodent – are among its favourite prey.

68 Some monkeys have a long tail that they use as an extra limb when climbing. This is called a prehensile tail. It contains a powerful system of bones and muscles so it can be used for gripping.

◀ Sloths live in Central and South American rainforests and swamps – they are surprisingly good swimmers.

66 The sloth hardly ever comes down to the ground. This jungle creature lives hanging from a branch by its special hook-like claws. It is so well adapted to this life that its fur grows downwards – the opposite way to that of most mammals – so that rainwater drips off more easily.

69 The okapi uses its long tongue to pick leaves from forest trees. This tongue is so long that the okapi can even lick its own eyes clean!

▶ Okapis feed in dense, remote rainforests in Central Africa.

67 Tapirs are pig–like animals that live on the jungle floor. There are three different kinds of tapir in the South American rainforests and one kind in the rainforests of Southeast Asia. Tapirs have long, bendy snouts and they feed on leaves, buds and grass.

◀ The Brazilian tapir is often found near water and is a good swimmer.

Strange foods

▼ The vampire bat feeds for about 30 minutes, and probably drinks about 26 litres of blood a year.

70 Some mammals only eat one or two kinds of food. The giant panda feeds mainly on the shoots and roots of the bamboo plant. It spends up to 12 hours a day eating, and consumes about 12 kilograms of bamboo a day. The panda also eats small amounts of other plants and sometimes hunts mice and fish.

▶ Giant pandas live in the bamboo forests of central China. There are very few pandas left in the wild, perhaps between 1500 and 3000.

71 The vampire bat feeds on blood — it is the only bat that has this special diet. This bat hunts at night. It finds a victim such as a horse or cow and crawls up its leg onto its body. The bat shaves away a small area of flesh and, using its long tongue, laps up blood that flows from the wound.

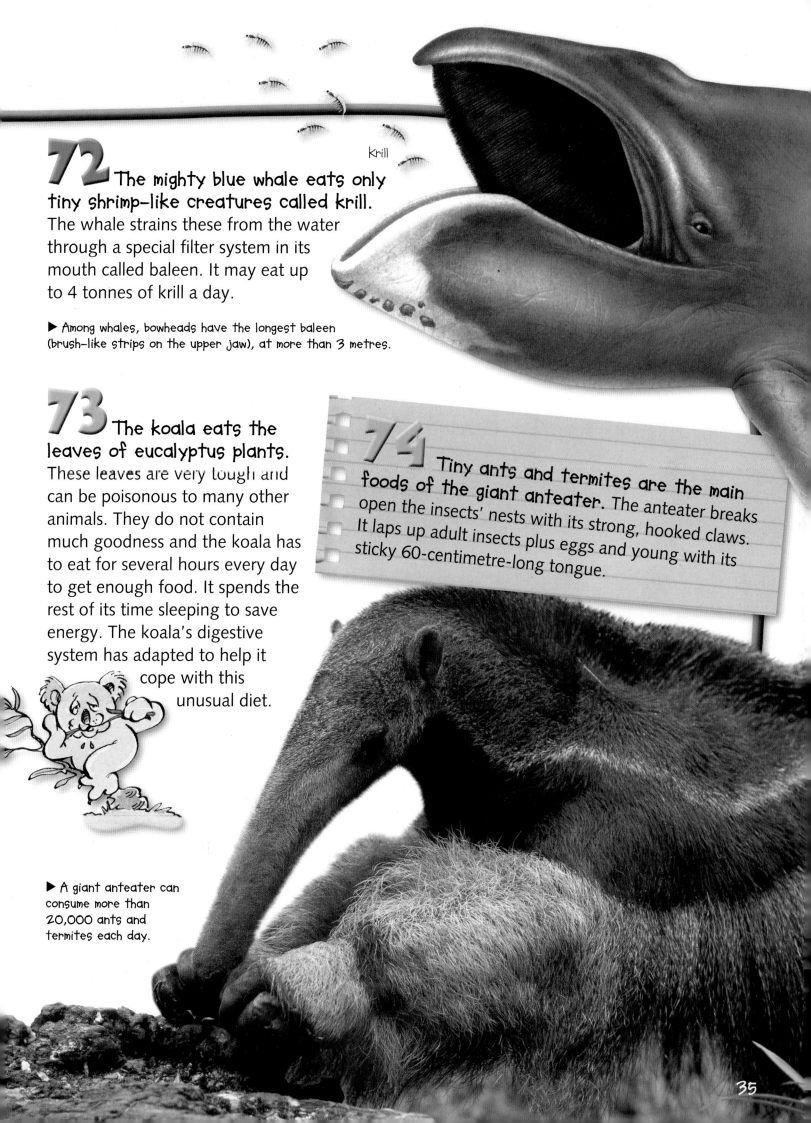

72 **The mighty blue whale eats only tiny shrimp-like creatures called krill.** The whale strains these from the water through a special filter system in its mouth called baleen. It may eat up to 4 tonnes of krill a day.

Krill

▶ Among whales, bowheads have the longest baleen (brush-like strips on the upper jaw), at more than 3 metres.

73 **The koala eats the leaves of eucalyptus plants.** These leaves are very tough and can be poisonous to many other animals. They do not contain much goodness and the koala has to eat for several hours every day to get enough food. It spends the rest of its time sleeping to save energy. The koala's digestive system has adapted to help it cope with this unusual diet.

74 **Tiny ants and termites are the main foods of the giant anteater.** The anteater breaks open the insects' nests with its strong, hooked claws. It laps up adult insects plus eggs and young with its sticky 60-centimetre-long tongue.

▶ A giant anteater can consume more than 20,000 ants and termites each day.

Tool users

75 The chimpanzee is one of the few mammals to use tools to help it find food. It uses a stone like a hammer to crack nuts, and makes use of sticks to pull down fruit from the trees and for fighting. It also uses sticks to help catch insects, for example, by jabbing them into holes in trees to get out grubs, moths and wild bee honey.

◀ The chimp pokes a sharp stick into a termite or ant nest. It waits a moment or two and then pulls the stick out, covered with juicy insects that it can eat.

I DON'T BELIEVE IT!

The cusimanse is a clever kind of mongoose. When it comes across a meal that has a tough shell, it throws it between its hind legs against a stone or tree to break it open and get at the tasty insides!

76 Dolphins show many kinds of intelligent behaviour, including tool use. Some dolphins tear bits of sea sponge from rocks and hold or place them over their snouts, then prod and probe among rocks and sand to find fish and other prey. The sponge prevents the dolphin scratching or hurting its snout.

▶ Dolphins that have learnt to use sponges swap skills with each other, and may even swap sponges.

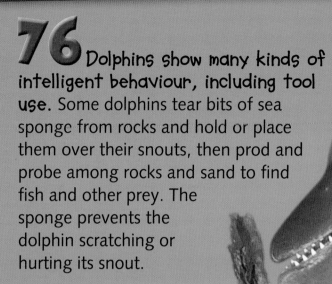

▼ A sea otter smashes a shellfish against a rock to get at the juicy flesh inside.

77 The sea otter uses a stone to break open its shellfish food. It feeds mainly on sea creatures with hard shells, such as mussels, clams and crabs. The sea otter lies on its back in the water and places a rock on its chest. It then bangs the shellfish against the rock until the shell breaks, allowing the otter to get at the soft flesh inside.

City creatures

78 Foxes are among the few larger mammals that manage to survive in towns and cities. They used to find their food in the countryside, but now more and more have discovered that city rubbish bins are a good hunting ground. The red fox will eat almost anything. It kills birds, rabbits, eats insects, fruit and berries and takes human leftovers.

I DON'T BELIEVE IT!

Rats will eat almost anything. They have been known to chew through electrical wires, lead piping and even concrete dams. In the US, rats may cause up to more than one billion dollars' worth of damage every year!

◄ The red fox has spread to all continents except South America and Antarctica, following humans as they throw away food refuse.

▼ The house mouse hides under floors and in cupboards. It will eat any human food it can find, as well as paper, glue and even soap!

79 Rats and mice are among the most successful of all mammals. They live all over the world and eat almost any kind of food. The brown rat and the house mouse are among the most common. The brown rat eats seeds, fruit and grain, but it will also attack birds and mice. In cities it lives in cellars and sewers – anywhere there is rotting food and rubbish.

▼ Young raccoons quickly learn to tip over rubbish bins and tear open plastic bags to get at meal leftovers.

80 Raccoons also live in city areas and raid rubbish bins for food. Like foxes, they eat lots of different kinds of food, including fish, nuts, seeds, berries and insects, as well as what they scavenge from humans. They are usually active at night and spend the day in a den made in a burrow, a hole in rocks or even in the corner of an empty city building.

Freshwater mammals

Among the best mammal swimmers are – elephants! They 'walk' in water without touching the bottom for hours and even go almost completely under, using their trunk as a snorkel.

81 Most river mammals spend only part of their time in water. Creatures such as the river otter and the water rat live on land and go into the water to find food. The hippopotamus, on the other hand, spends most of its day in water to keep cool. Its skin needs to stay moist, and it cracks if it gets too dry.

82 At night hippos leave their river or lake to chomp on land plants. However they rarely stray far and gallop back to water if danger threatens.

83 The water vole makes its home in a bankside burrow. It eats plants growing near the water and in the shallows, and is an expert swimmer.

▲ The water vole has a blunt nose, and furry ears and tail, unlike the brown rat, for which it is often mistaken.

84 The platypus uses its duck-like beak to find food on the riverbed. This strange beak is extremely sensitive to touch and to tiny electric currents given off by prey. The platypus dives down to the bottom of the river and digs in the mud for creatures such as worms and shrimps.

◄ When a platypus has found its food, it stores it in its cheeks until it has time to eat it.

85 The otter's ears close off when it is swimming. This stops water getting into them when the otter dives. Other special features are webbed feet, and short, thick fur, which keeps the otter's skin dry.

▼ The hippo is not a good swimmer but it can walk on the riverbed. It can stay underwater for up to half an hour.

86 Most dolphins are sea creatures but some live in rivers. There are four different kinds of river dolphins living in rivers in Asia and South America. The baiji of China is now considered to be extinct. All feed on fish and shellfish. They probably use echolocation, a kind of sonar like that used by bats, to find their prey.

Plant-eaters

87 **In order to get enough nourishment, plant-eaters must spend much of their time eating.** A zebra spends at least half its day munching grass. The advantage of being a plant-eater, though, is that the animal does not have to chase and compete for its food like hunters do.

▼ The Mexican long-tongued bat flaps its wings fast to hover in front of flowers as it feeds.

88 **Some kinds of bat feed on pollen and nectar.** The Queensland blossom bat, for example, has a long brush-like tongue that it plunges deep into flowers to gather its food. As it feeds it pollinates the flowers – it takes the male pollen to the female parts of a flower so that it can bear seeds and fruits.

▼ Carnivores, such as lions, feed on plant-eaters, such as zebras. So there must always be more plant-eaters than carnivores for this 'food chain' to work successfully.

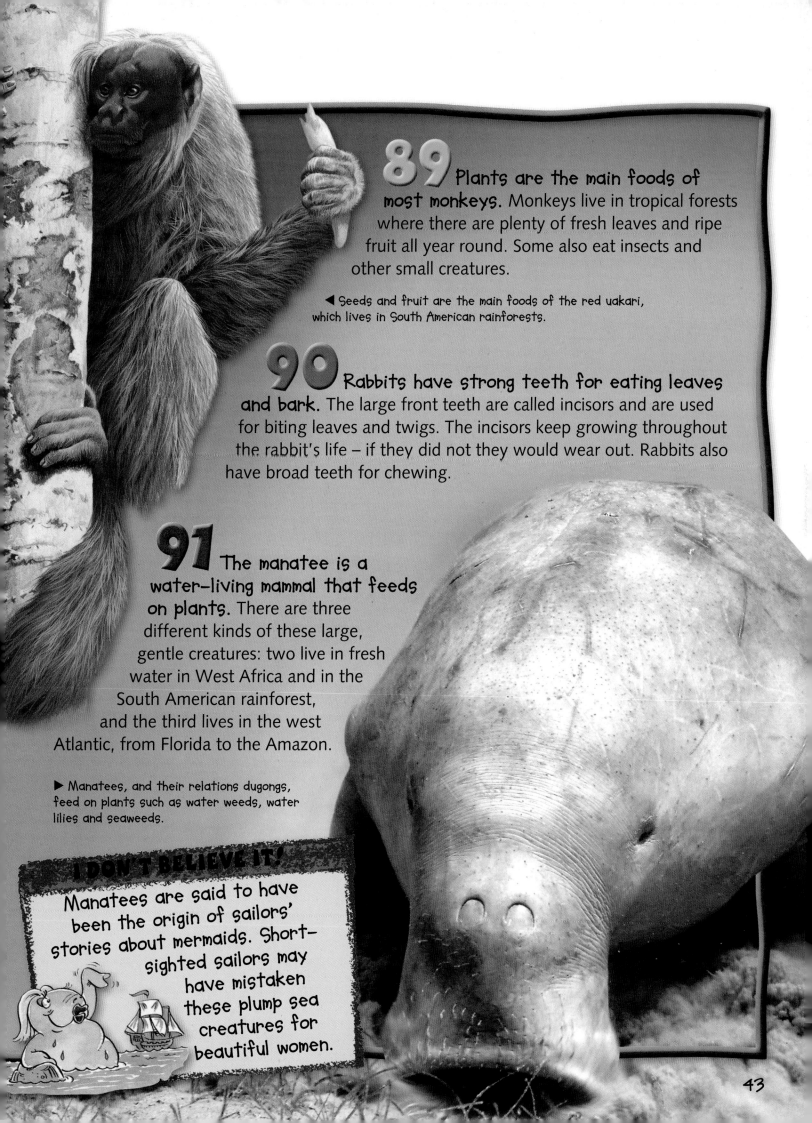

89 Plants are the main foods of most monkeys. Monkeys live in tropical forests where there are plenty of fresh leaves and ripe fruit all year round. Some also eat insects and other small creatures.

◀ Seeds and fruit are the main foods of the red uakari, which lives in South American rainforests.

90 Rabbits have strong teeth for eating leaves and bark. The large front teeth are called incisors and are used for biting leaves and twigs. The incisors keep growing throughout the rabbit's life – if they did not they would wear out. Rabbits also have broad teeth for chewing.

91 The manatee is a water-living mammal that feeds on plants. There are three different kinds of these large, gentle creatures: two live in fresh water in West Africa and in the South American rainforest, and the third lives in the west Atlantic, from Florida to the Amazon.

▶ Manatees, and their relations dugongs, feed on plants such as water weeds, water lilies and seaweeds.

I DON'T BELIEVE IT!

Manatees are said to have been the origin of sailors' stories about mermaids. Short-sighted sailors may have mistaken these plump sea creatures for beautiful women.

43

Digging deep

KEY

1 Anti-flood wall around entrance
2 Side chamber
3 Food store
4 Members greet by 'kissing'
5 Nursery chamber
6 Rest/sleep chamber

92 **Prairie dogs are champion burrowers.** These little animals are a kind of plump short-tailed squirrel. There are five different species, and all live in North America. They dig large burrows, which contain several chambers linked by tunnels.

I DON'T BELIEVE IT!

Prairie dogs are not always safe underground. Sometimes burrowing owls move into part of a burrow and then prey on the prairie dogs already living there.

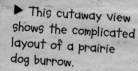

▶ This cutaway view shows the complicated layout of a prairie dog burrow.

93 Badgers dig a network of chambers and tunnels called a sett. There are special areas for breeding, sleeping and food stores. Sleeping areas are lined with dry grass and leaves, which the badgers sometimes take outside to air for a while.

▼ Badgers usually stay in their burrow during the day and come out at dusk. They are playful creatures and adults are often seen playing with their cubs.

▼ The star-nosed mole's sensitive feelers find prey by touch.

94 Moles have specially adapted front feet for digging. The feet are broad and turn outward for pushing through the soil, and the claws are large and strong. Moles have very poor sight. Their sense of touch is well developed and they has sensitive bristles on their faces.

Mothers and babies

95 Most whales are born tail first. If the baby emerged head first it could drown during the birth process. As soon as the baby has fully emerged, the mother, with the help of other females, gently pushes it up to the surface to take its first breath. The female whale feeds her baby on milk, just like other mammals.

▼ For the first months of its life, a young whale, such as this grey whale calf, remains almost touching its mother.

96 Whales are the biggest of all mammal babies. A newborn grey whale is 4 metres long, weighs two-thirds of a tonne, and drinks 200 litres of its mother's milk every day – over two bathtubs full!

97 The Virginia opossum may have more than 15 babies at one time – more than any other mammal. The young are only a centimetre long, and all of the babies together weigh only a couple of grams.

98 Bears have some of the smallest babies, compared to the mother's size, of all placental mammals. A newborn giant panda weighs just 120 grams, while its mother can weigh up to 120 kilograms – 1000 times heavier. The length of pregnancy for the mother sloth bear is about seven months. Like other bears, she usually has just one or two offspring in each litter.

◄ A mother sloth bear carries her young on her back until they are perhaps one year old.

100 Baby mammals needs lots of care. The young of many hunting mammals, from tiny weasels to wolves, bears and the biggest cats, are born furless, helpless, and unable to see and hear properly. The mother keeps them safe in a nest or den and returns between hunting to provide milk.

99 Some babies have to be up and running less than an hour after birth. If the young of animals such as antelopes were as helpless as the baby panda they would immediately be snapped up by predators. They must get to their feet and be able to move with the herd as quickly as possible or they will not survive.

► A newborn bison struggles to its feet minutes after birth – wolves or cougars may be near.

Index

Page numbers in **bold** refer to main subject entries. Those in *italics* refer to illustrations.